The Hospice Experience

making your most important final decisions

by
Othniel J. Seiden, MD
&
Jane L. Bilett, Ph.D.

Cover Art
by Capri Brock

A Books To Believe In Publication
All Rights Reserved
Copyright 2008 by Othniel J. Seiden & Jane L. Bilett

Proudly Published by
Thornton Publishing, Inc
17011 Lincoln Ave. #408
Parker, CO 80134

www.BooksToBelieveIn.com

Phone: 303.794.8888
Fax: 720.863.2013

www.BooomerBookSeries.com

ISBN: 0-9801941-5-6

Dedicated to all
hospice staff members
and especially their
wonderful volunteers…

Thanks to you all!

CONTENTS

Purpose of This Book 8
Making the decision...

1. History of Hospice 10
How did it all get started?

2. When Should Hospice Be Considered? 15
What are the indications?

3. Finding a Hospice for Your Needs 20
Picking the right facility...

.
4. What Questions Should Be Asked? 23
It's important you get all
the fact to be satisfied...

5. What Is the Function of Hospice? 27
What you have the right to expect...

.
6. Home Hospice 29
What to expect with home hospice...

.
7. Hospice Facility Care 32
What to expect from in patient care...

8. The Hospice Team **39**
Some of the most remarkable
people you'll ever meet...

9. Hospice Care for the Patient **45**
It's all about the patient...

10. Hospice Care for the Family **46**
Family, friends and loved
ones will find support too...

11. Hospice Care for Children **49**
Care and support for the child patient
or the child survivor of a dying parent...

12. Being a Caregiver **52**
One of the hardest jobs you'll ever have...

13. After It's Over **57**
No matter how prepared you are,
you're never ready...

14. Bereavement **59**
Grief is a difficult job
you mustn't avoid it...

15. Facing Life **62**
After the grief has been
worked through engage in the
renewed life your loved one
would want you to live...

Purpose of This Book

Making the Decision...

Making the decision to use hospice is perhaps the most important final decision you may ever make. The availability of hospice is a blessing to those who avail themselves of the service in their final days, weeks or months. It is also a service to help their families and loved ones. However, as wonderful as hospice and its services are, the decision to use hospice is not a simple one. It is, by its very nature, is an emotionally difficult decision to make.

It is the purpose of this book

- ❖ to help the patient and his/her family to make that decision with a clear understanding of what they should expect
- ❖ highlight what the pros and cons of hospice are, which ones are might be the most significant for them
- ❖ show them how to choose the best services to serve their personal needs.

Our qualifications for writing this book are both from clinical and personal experience. Jane's expertise comes from over 30 years in private practice in clinical psychology, and her experience dealing with the stresses of patients and their families facing their terminal time and the grief that follows for those family members and loved ones who must move on after the loss of their loved one.

Othniel's expertise is two fold, through over 40 years of medical practice, advising patients and their families in making their final decisions and more important, from the knowledge he gained when his mother-in-law entered hospice and five years later when his own wife of 48 years entered hospice at the end of her battle with lung cancer.

We hope that our combined years of experiences with hospice will help you make an educated decision with full knowledge of what you should expect from the decision you make. As wonderful as hospice services are, hospice is not for everyone.

A further decision you will have to make if hospice service is selected will be whether to use home hospice or enter a hospice facility. Both have their advantages and disadvantages.

No hospice decision is easy; hopefully we can help you over the hurdles.

I

History of Hospice

How did it all get started?

The basic idea of hospice is centuries old, growing out of the care given to the sick and dying in European and Middle Eastern monasteries where monks gave palliative treatment and end of life care to the dying fortunate enough to avail themselves of their services.

The term *"hospice"* itself comes from the root "hospitality" can be traced back to medieval times when it referred to a place of shelter and rest for weary or ill travelers on a long journey.

The name was first applied to specialized care for dying patients by Mme Jeanne Garnier who founded the Dames de Calaire in Lyon, France, in 1842. The name was next introduced by the Irish Sisters of Charity when they opened Our Lady's Hospice in Dublin in 1879 and St Joseph's Hospice in Hackney, London (1905).

Most credit for the modern concept of hospice is given to the British physician Dame Cicely Saunders, who founded the first modern hospice — St.

Christopher's Hospice — in a residential suburb of London in 1967. Dame Cicely Saunders was a physician, who earlier trained as a social worker as well as a nurse. Not only did she found the first modern hospice program, she compounded a mixture of several pain medications to be known as Brompton's Cocktail. But she also realized that this elixir for physical pain was not enough for the dying and their loved ones, so in collaboration with Stanislaus Graf, a psychologist, they developed a holistic psychological, social and spiritual program for the relief of psychological, emotional and spiritual sufferings of their patients and families.

Dr. Saunders introduced the idea of specialized care for the dying to the United States, four years before opening her own hospice. She was visiting Yale University in 1963 for a lecture given to medical students, nurses, social workers, and chaplains. The talk she gave was about her concept of holistic hospice care, of terminally ill cancer patients and their families. Her moving lecture launched a chain of events, resulting in the development of hospice care as we know it today.

In 1965, Florence Wald, then the Dean of the Yale School of Nursing, invited Saunders to return and become a visiting faculty member of the school for the spring term. Turn about being fair play, in 1968 Florence Wald took a sabbatical from Yale to work at St. Christopher's to learn all she could about hospice.

In 1969, Dr. Elisabeth Kubler-Ross published her book *On Death and Dying*, based on more than 500 interviews with dying patients. It identified the five stages which most terminally ill patients passed. The book immediately became an internationally known best seller.

In the book, Kubler-Ross encouraged home care as opposed to treatment in an institutional settings and arguing that patients should have a choice and ability to participate in the decisions that affect their remaining time.

In 1972, Dr. Kubler-Ross testified at the first national hearings on the subject of "Death with Dignity," which was conducted at the U.S. Senate Special Committee on Aging. Dr. Kubler-Ross testified, "We live in a very particular death-denying society. We isolate both the dying and the old, and it serves a purpose. They are reminders of our own mortality. We should not institutionalize people. We can give families more help with home care and visiting nurses, giving the families and the patients the spiritual, emotional, and financial help in order to facilitate the final care at home."

In 1974, this led to the enactment of the first hospice legislation introduced by Senators Frank Church and Frank E. Moss to provide federal funds for hospice programs.

In 1978, a U.S. Department of Health, Education, and Welfare task force reported, "the hospice movement as a concept for the care of the terminally ill and their families is a viable concept and one which holds out a means of providing more humane care for Americans dying of terminal illness while possibly reducing costs. As such, it is the proper subject of federal support."

In 1979, The Health Care Financing Administration (HCFA) initiated demonstration programs at 26 hospices across the country assessing the cost effectiveness of hospice care and to determine what a hospice should provide.

Following this, in 1980, the W.K. Kellogg Foundation awarded a grant to the Joint Commission on Accreditation of Hospitals (JCAHO) to investigate the status of hospice and to develop standards for hospice accreditation.

Most importantly in 1982, Congress included a provision to create a Medicare hospice benefit.

In 1984, JCAHO initiated hospice accreditation.

In 1986, States were given the option of including hospice in their Medicaid programs. Hospice care became available to terminally ill nursing home residents.

In 1993, hospice was included as a nationally guaranteed benefit under President Clinton's health care reform proposal. Hospice is now an accepted part of the health care continuum.

In 1996, The Ninth U.S. Circuit Court of Appeals in San Francisco overruled a Washington State Law against physician-assisted suicide. The Second US Circuit Court of Appeals struck down New York's law against physician-assisted suicide. Both rulings were appealed to the US Supreme Court.

In 1997, Congress passed legislation barring taxpayer dollars from financing physician-assisted suicide. The US Supreme Court rules that mentally competent terminally ill people do not have a constitutional right to physician-assisted suicide, leaving the issue up to the states. Oregon voters affirm the right to physician-assisted suicide by passing for the second time its "Death with Dignity Act." The growing end-of-life movement focused national attention on quality of life at the end of life as well as the need for increased public awareness and physician education. The hospice philosophy and concept of care is central to models for palliative and end-of-life care.

In February of 1999, the U.S. Postal Service issued the Hospice Care commemorative stamp. Today hospice care is widely accepted throughout the United States and most of the world.

II

When Should Hospice Be Considered?

What are the indications?

Preparation for Inevitable Approaching Death

Death occurs when the when the spirit completes its natural process of reconciling and the body completes its natural process of physically shutting down. These two processes occur uniquely to the values, beliefs, and lifestyle of the dying person. Thus, the first indication for turning to hospice is the desire by the dying person. He/she must make the decision that no further treatment efforts are desired; that only palliative and comfort therapy be administered. The second indication in most states is that the patient's physician affirms that the life expectancy of the patient is no longer than six month in spite of any therapy available for treatment of the terminal illness.

On the physical plane, death approaches when the body begins the final process of shutting down, ending when all the physical systems cease to function. This is usually an orderly, progressive series of physical changes. They are a normal and natural way in which the body prepares itself to stop. When the patient and physician agree that most appropriate treatment should be limited to comfort enhancing measures, it is the indication to consider entering hospice.

Palliative physical pain relief is not the only therapy to be sought. The emotional-spiritual-mental plane must be addressed. The spiritual and mental processes of the dying person beginning to prepare for its passing. This process also follows its own priorities, which include the resolution of any unfinished business and gaining permission to "let go" from family members. The goal of hospice is to support the emotional-spiritual-mental changes to ease and facilitate this transition. When a person's body is physically ready and even wanting to stop, to shut down and bring an end to physical discomfort, but the emotional is still unresolved, not reconciled over some issue or significant relationship, he/she may linger in order to resolve whatever needs finishing. Likewise, when a person is emotionally, spiritually or mentally resolved and ready for passing on, but the physical body has not completed its physical shut down the person will continue to live until that ending process is completed.

So when should a decision about entering a hospice program be made and who should make it? Discussion of the patient's care options is appropriate at any time during a life-limiting illness. Remember, by law the decision belongs to the patient. Most hospices accept patients who have a life-expectancy of six months or less and who are referred by their personal physician. The patient and his/her family should feel free to discuss hospice care at any time with their physician, any health care professionals, clergy or friends. This conversation may be initiated by the physician, but it is certainly not necessary to wait for a health care professional to bring up the subject. Though most health care professionals and clergy know about hospice, if you or they require or want more information about hospice, it is readily available from the National Council of Hospice Professionals Physician Section, medical societies, state hospice organizations, or the National Hospice Helpline, 1-800-658-8898. Further information about hospice can be obtained from the American Cancer Society, the American Association of Retired Persons, and the Social Security Administration.

It should also be understood that minds and wishes can always be changed. Should the patient's condition improve or the disease goes into remission, patients can always be discharged from hospice and return to aggressive therapy or return to their daily life. If at a later date the discharged patient should need to return to hospice care, Medicare and most private insurance will allow additional coverage for that purpose.

So how is the hospice admission process achieved?

Once the hospice is contacted, they will in turn, contact the patient's physician making sure he/she agrees that hospice care is appropriate at this time. The patient will then be asked to sign consent and insurance forms. These are similar to the forms patients sign when entering a hospital. The "hospice election form" says that the patient understands that the care is palliative, aimed only at pain relief and symptom control rather than curative. It also outlines the services available. The form Medicare patients sign also tells how electing the Medicare hospice benefit affects other Medicare coverage. When this is done, the patient is then admitted to hospice care either in the hospice facility or for hospice home care.

When Othniel's mother-in-law decided to go into hospice after a six month fight with lung cancer, her decision was quite sudden. She'd been through all the therapies available to her, both radiation and chemo. She was on oxygen and any activity exhausted her. Her oncologist suggested that another course of chemo could be tried, but that there was little chance that it would be helpful. She turned to Othniel's first wife and him and said, "I'm just so tired of this. The thought of going through any more treatment that will probably futile… it just isn't worth it too me. I've had all the suffering I can stand. I just want to be left in peace…" After some further discussion with her doctor she decided then and there that she wanted to go into hospice. She passed away comfortably after just two weeks and several times stated that she wished she'd made the decision earlier to give up the struggle and suffering.

Six years later, Othniel's first wife faced the same

struggle with lung cancer. This after she'd survived breast cancer for over nine years. She underwent surgery to remove the tumor and a portion of her lung, and then had a course of radiation and two courses of chemo. Her physical condition deteriorated over two years until she too decided it was futile to continue further treatments. She, like her mother, decided she no longer wanted to prolong her slowly dying and elected to settle for palliative and comfort treatment for the final time she had left. That remaining time turned out to be twelve weeks spent in hospice. She never seemed to regret her decision.

III

Finding a Hospice for Your Needs

Picking the right facility...

Choosing the right hospice is one of the most important decisions you'll have to make; however, this is only an issue if there is more than one hospice in your area. If you live in a fairly large metropolitan area, there will probably be several hospices to choose from. If you know anyone who has utilized a hospice in your area, ask them about their experience. A good reference from someone you know and trust who used hospice is probably your best and most reliable sources of information. But remember, needs vary, so even these references should be evaluated with your situation and concerns in mind. The best way to discover how many hospices exist in your local area is to look in the yellow pages under "hospice." Also your physician any clergy can give you a list and probably opinions of their care and services, but consider their opinions with your needs in mind. They may make recommendations because of a hospices church affiliation or relationship to a certain hospital rather than by consideration of your needs. Your job is to gather as much information as you can about all hospices available to you and then decide which is best for your needs.

Size of the hospice is no indication of its quality care. A large hospice may be able to pay for advertisements, but that does not necessarily make them better hospices. Belonging to a national, state or local hospice organization does not make it superior to unaffiliated hospices in the area. Hospices may choose not to join organizations, because they don't care to pay fees and dues to the organization which may offer them no benefits. A better indicator of quality is to find out if the hospice is accredited by an organization such as "JCOAHO" or the Joint Commission On Accreditation Of Healthcare Organizations. By being accredited by JCOAHO, a hospice agrees to inspections by JCOAHO and must meet higher standards of care than hospices who are not JCOAHO accredited. Again, many small hospices provide excellent care, often more personal care with individual needs in mind. Asking your physician for the names of all hospices in the area is a good place to start, and it might be a good idea to contact a social worker or the discharge planner at one of your local hospitals.

If someone gives you a specific reference or referral to a particular hospice, be sure to ask for reasons why the hospice is thought to be better than the others in your area. Remember, individual and family needs differ dramatically. Openly discuss your needs with your physician, who is ultimately going to be in charge of your or your loved ones care in hospice. .

Visiting as many hospice facilities and speaking with the staff is a very good idea. Ask how many patients each nurse takes care of on a shift. Observe for yourself how clean the facility. Speak with the families of patients at each of the facilities and determine how happy they are with the care, the food, the compassion of the staff.

By law, each State inspects, licenses and certifies hospices to assure that they meet the uniform standards of care set by law in Federal and State regulations for hospices. When inspections are performed, a survey summary is written and must be made available to the public. Ask for the phone number and address of your State's Freedom of Information Office and ask to receive a copy of the survey summaries for the most recent inspection of the hospices in your area and especially a copy of any inspections performed as a result of any complaints filed with the Department.

Choosing the right hospice for your specific needs, the patient's specific needs, is the most important step in keeping your loved one comfortable. Continue to keep fully informed about the care and services to which you are entitled to receive and always clearly communicate your wishes to assure you are getting the very best care.

IV

What Questions Should Be Asked?

It's important you get all the fact to be satisfied...

When you've narrowed your decision down as to which hospices you are considering, there are some questions you might ask before you make your final selection. The following questions are ones you should consider asking with the answers you should expect.

How will this hospice manage pain?

Keep in mind that emotional and spiritual pain is as real as physical pain and in need of attention, so both should be addressed. The answers you get should make you satisfied that the hospice nurses and doctors are up to date on the best methods, medications and devices for pain and symptom relief. Ask about their success rate in battling pain. By using combinations of medications, various therapies and counseling most patients should attain a very high and acceptable level of comfort.

What other services are available here?

In addition, physical and occupational therapists can assist patients to be as mobile and self-sufficient as they wish or is possible. However realize that some hospice patients may prefer to be left to rest and should never be coerced to participate in any activities they don't desire. Often specialists in music therapy, art therapy, massage and diet counseling and other activities are available to help the patient fill time and relieve stress. In addition, social and psychological counselors and clergy are available to assist patients and family members as well. Again, make sure that the activity level of the patient will be selected by the patient and never forced. Some hospice patients want nothing more than to be able to sleep pain free.

With all the medications, will the patient be able to communicate and know what's going on?

Yes, in most cases. The goal of hospice is to have the patient as comfortable and pain free as well as alert as possible. By constantly consulting with the patient, and understanding his/her wishes, hospices are very successful in accomplishing this goal.

Is this hospice affiliated with any religious organization?

While some churches and religious groups have started hospices frequently in partnership with their hospitals, they do not require patients to adhere to any religion or particular set of beliefs. You should be able to have your own clergy visit regardless of religion and not be bothered by clergy if so desired.

Will this hospice care covered by insurance?

Hospice insurance coverage is widely accepted. Coverage is provided by Medicare nationwide, by Medicaid in 47 states, as well as by most private insurance providers. To be assured of coverage, families should check with their employer or health insurance agent or provider.

If Medicare eligible, are there any additional expenses not covered?

Medicare Hospice Benefits cover the full scope of medical and support services needed to comfort for a life-limiting illness. Hospice care also should support the family and loved ones of the person through a variety of services. This benefit covers almost all aspects of hospice care with little further expense to the patient or family.

If we have no health insurance what services can hospice provide?

Most hospices will try to provide those who cannot pay by funds raised from the community or if available, from memorial or foundation gifts. However, the first thing hospices do is to assist families in finding out if the patient is eligible for coverage they may not be aware of.

What services, if any, does this hospice provide to the family after the patient passes on?

Most hospices continue contact and support for family and children of the diseased for at least a year and often more if needed, following the death of a loved one. Most also sponsor bereavement groups and support for anyone in the community who has experienced the death of a family member or a close friend.

V

What Is the Function of Hospice?

What you have the right to expect...

Today's hospices should offer a patent and his/her family a complete program of care for the patients and support for families facing a life ending illness. Furthermore, hospice is a concept of care, not necessarily a place of care, as in most cases home hospice is an option. Home hospice will be covered in greater detail in the next chapter.

Whereas hospitals emphasize treatment of diseases, hospice emphasizes and limits its care to palliative rather than curative treatment. Hospice's goal is to maintain the best possible quality of life rather than extending quantity of life. Professional medical care is given aimed at sophisticated symptom relief and providing maximum physical and psychological comfort for the patient.. The patient and his/her family are both included in the care and both emotional and spiritual support is offered based on the patient's wishes and the family's needs. Usually well trained volunteers offer relief for family members, allowing them to leave as needed knowing the patient's needs will continue to be satisfied. Hospice regards dying as a normal life process. Hospice does nothing to hasten death nor does it postpone death. Hospice provides the specific personalized services so their patients and their families can attain a death that is as comfortable physically and emotionally as possible for them. Families and patients involved in the dying process have a many different physical, spiritual and emotional needs. The goal of the hospice team is to be sensitive and responsive to the special requirements and unique needs of each individual and family.

Hospices accept anyone regardless of age or type of illness who has only a limited life expectancy and has made a decision to spend their last months of life without further treatment of their disease but rather at peace and limiting their treatment to attain maximum physical and emotional comfort. Their choice is to achieve this treatment either at home or in a hospice facility.

VI

Home Hospice

What to expect with home hospice...

It is not surprising that many patients wish to spend their last days in the familiar surroundings of their home. For them, home hospice is frequently a viable option. In these situations, your chosen hospice provider will come to your home to assess your specific needs, recommend any special supplies you may need, and help make arrangements to obtain any necessary equipment. Early on, the need for equipment may be minimal, increasing as the illness progresses. Usually your hospice will assist you in any way it can to make home care as simple, convenient, clean and safe as possible.

Very often, hospice can be started out at home and when the situation becomes too difficult for the patient or caregivers it can be transferred to the hospice facility. The converse is also possible where the patient starts out in the hospice facility and if the caregiver or family gains sufficient confidence, the transfer can be made to home hospice. Any consideration should be given to the patient's wishes and carried out if at all possible.

The major burden of caregiving in home hospice will necessarily fall upon family and friends. There's no set number of people necessary to give home care as this depends and differs with each case. To determine the amount of care needed in each case the hospice team should prepare a specific individualized care plan that will address the amount of caregiving needed by the patient. Hospice staff will visit regularly and should always be accessible to answer medical questions, provide support, and teach caregivers their necessary skills.

Often in the early weeks of home care, it may not be necessary for someone to be with the patient at all times; but since one of the most common fears of patients is that of dying alone, hospice generally recommends someone be there continuously as the end time draws near. Though family and friends do deliver most of the care in home hospice, the facility provide volunteers to assist with errands and to provide a break and time away for the primary caregivers. Family and friends often have guilt feelings over being away during this time, but you have to keep in mind that constant care causes stress and burnout and it is important that caregivers take breaks and time for themselves.

Keep in mind that it is never easy and sometimes can be quite difficult taking care of a dying person at home. It is especially difficult if a great deal of custodial care is needed or if the patient is not ambulatory. Toward the end of a long and progressive illness, nights especially can be very difficult, lonely and frightening. For this reason, hospice staff should be available around the clock for phone consultation with the family and to make night visits when appropriate. Providing family members with volunteer companionship is another service of hospice during this stressful and lonely time.

Hospice provides home-based patients many of the services available to in facility patient care. Home based hospice patients are served by a team of physicians, physician's assistants, nurses, social workers, counselors, hospice certified nursing assistants, clergy, therapists, and many volunteers. Of course hospices provide medications, supplies, equipment, and hospital services, related to the terminal illness.

Always keep in mind that hospice patients can receive care not only in their homes but in nursing homes, hospital hospice units and inpatient hospice centers.

VII

Hospice Facility Care

What to expect during hospice patient care...

Of course all the services hospice offers to caregivers during out-of-facility care are offered in the inpatient program. Nothing is done to speed the death process, but treatments are designed to keep the patient comfortable and at peace. The main difference with inpatient care is that a greater part of the burden of care is shifted from family to the hospice staff. Inpatient care is given in a quiet, peaceful, pleasant environment usually designed to look as little as possible like institutional surroundings. You will probably be encouraged to bring pictures and knick knacks that are of value to the patient to help give a feeling of home and familiarity.

Prepare yourself for the progression of signs and symptoms you will have to witness as the patient approaches his/her final moments. The emotional, spiritual, mental and physical changes of impending death described herein are offered to you to understand the natural progression of life ending events. Of course, not all of these signs and symptoms will be seen with every patient, nor will they necessarily occur in this exact sequence in all cases. The following describes how the body prepares itself for the final stage of life.

Change in the patient's skin color and coolness to the touch of his/her hands arms, feet and then legs may be first noticed and they may become increasingly cool with time. This is a normal progression and an indication that the circulation of blood is slowing and decreasing to the body's extremities. The blood is actually being shunted to the most vital organs. Of course, if the illness is accompanied by fever this may not be evident. Keep the patient comfortably warm with a blanket or sweater.

Sleep may increase, the patient spending an increasing amount of time napping. He/she may be more and more uncommunicative and unresponsive, and at times might be difficult to arouse. This is due, in part, to changes in metabolism as the body slows and begins to shut down. At such times, it is still comforting to the patient to sit with your loved one and hold his/her hand. You can and should speak softly and naturally to the patient. Assume you are being heard. You should only speak of pleasant or comforting things in the company of the sleeping patient. You may be surprised just how much they hear and understand when you think them in deep slumber. Spend as much time as possible with your loved one during times when he/she seems awake and is most alert. Talk about the person away from the person's presence.

Always assume the person can hear you!!! Hearing is the last of the senses lost.

As time passes, the patient may seem to be confused about the time, place, and even the identity of people surrounding him/her often including close and familiar people. This is due in part to the slowed blood circulation and metabolic changes. If there seems to be confusion, identify yourself by name before you speak rather than asking the person to guess who you are. Speak softly, clearly, and truthfully when you need to communicate something.

Incontinence is one of the most distressing parts of caregiving and also a point of discomfort and embarrassment to the patient. The person may lose control of urine and/or bowels as the muscles in that area begin to relax. Discuss with your hospice nurse or other staff, what can be done to protect the bed and keep your loved one clean and comfortable. There are a number of products on the market to help keep the work of caring for incontinence to a minimum.

Another difficult part of hygiene care is airway maintenance. Congestion may cause the patient to have gurgling sounds coming from his/her chest. These sounds may become quite loud. This change is due to the decrease of fluid intake and an inability to cough up normal secretions. Suctioning usually only increases the secretions and causes sharp discomfort and should be used as a last necessary resort. It is better to gently turn the person's head to the side allowing gravity to drain the secretions and gently wipe the mouth with a moist cloth.

Restlessness may be recognized during waking moments of the patient. He/she may display restless and repetitive motions such as pulling at bed linen or clothing, thrashing about in bed and not seeming to be able to stay still. This is due in part to the decrease in oxygen circulation to the brain and to metabolic changes. Instead of restraining such actions, to have a calming effect, speak in a quiet, natural way, lightly massage the forehead, read to the person, or play some soothing music. The staff may at this time start the patient on a mild oxygen flow.

Due to the patient's reduced fluid intake his/her urine output will decrease and become concentrated turning dark and tea colored. This may also be a sign of decrease in circulation through the kidneys. The eventual decrease in fluid and food is quite normal. There will probably be a decrease in appetite and thirst, wanting little or no food or fluid. The body is beginning to conserve energy which is expended on these tasks. Do not force food or drink into the person, or try to use guilt to manipulate them into eating or drinking more. Small chips of ice, frozen Gatorade or juice may be refreshing in the mouth. If the person is able to swallow, fluids may be given in small amounts by syringe. Glycerin swabs may help keep the mouth and lips moist, fresh and comfortable. Sucking on a cool, moist washcloth may help with oral comfort and hygiene and a moist cloth on the forehead may also increase physical comfort.

Cheyne-Stokes breathing is a breathing pattern change you may notice as time grows shorter. The patient's regular breathing pattern may change to a different breathing pace. This particular pattern consists of breathing irregularly, with shallow breaths and periods of no breathing of five to thirty seconds and sometimes up to a full minute.

The patient may also experience periods of rapid shallow panting breathing. These patterns are common but disturbing to the observer and indicate decrease in circulation to the internal organs. Elevating the head, and/or turning the person onto his/her side may bring comfort. Oxygen may be prescribed for comfort. Remain calm and speak comfortingly to your loved one.

Withdrawal is almost inevitable from time to time during these last days or weeks. The patient may seem unresponsive and withdrawn, sometimes even in a comatose-like state. This may indicate his/her preparation for release, a detaching from surroundings and relationships; it's a beginning of letting go. As mentioned before, since hearing remains all the way to the end, speak to your loved one in your normal tone of voice, identifying yourself by name when you speak, hold his/her hand, and say whatever you need to say that will help the person let go. Tell the patient it's okay to let go and pass on; that you understand. It will ease his/her task.

Delusional or vision-like experiences are not uncommon and you should be prepared for them. The patient may speak or claim to have spoken to persons who have already died, or to see or have seen places not visible to you. This does not indicate a hallucination or a drug reaction. The person is beginning to detach from this life and is preparing for the transition to death so it will not be frightening. Rather than contradicting, belittling or arguing about what the person claims to have seen or heard, accept their experience. Be agreeable, it is real to your loved one so affirm his/her experience; they are very normal and common.

There may come a time of decreased socialization. The patient may want to be with a very few or perhaps just one person. This is a late sign of preparation for release and affirms from whom the support is most needed in order to make the transition. If you are not included in this inner circle at the end, do not feel hurt for it does not mean you are not loved or are unimportant. It means you have already fulfilled your task with your loved one, and it's your time to say good-bye. If you are part of the final inner circle, the person still needs your affirmation, support, and permission to pass. Give your permission and understanding.

It can be very difficult to give your permission to your loved one to let go. It must be done without making him/her guilty for leaving. Don't try to keep him/her with you to meet your own needs. A dying person may try to hold on, even though it brings prolonged discomfort, in order to be sure those who are going to be left behind will be all right. Your ability to release the dying person from this concern and giving him/her assurance that it is all right to let go whenever he/she is ready is one of the greatest gifts you will ever have to give your loved one. Often a patient will hang on waiting for a loved one to come so he/she can have closure. Explain that if he/she is ready to pass you will verbalize his/her feelings and thus allow the patient to pass in peace.

Saying good-bye is difficult but necessary... When the person is ready to die, you must be able to let go. This is the time to say good-bye. Saying good-bye is your final gift of love to your loved one and is important to both of you. It gives closure to both of you and makes the final release possible. Say everything you need to say. It could be as simple as saying, I love you or it may include recounting favorite memories and activities you shared. Perhaps a simple but heartfelt, "Thank you for a wonderful shared life," is all that need be said. It's a time when tears need not be hidden from your loved one. Tears express your love and help you to let go.

VIII

The Hospice Team

Some of the most remarkable people you'll ever meet...

Hospice staff is made up of very special people. They are remarkable in that they work under very stressful conditions in an environment that would be most depressing to most people, yet they turn the situation into as positive an experience for their patients and the attending families and friends as is humanly possible. They have extraordinary compassion, empathy, acceptance of all lifestyles of their patients and their families, are non-judgmental and respectful of those they attend, have a gentleness of spirit, great humility, and an encouraging spirit.Above all they are totally honest with their patients answering their needs and questions and helping them make the best of their situation.

The Hospice Physician
Though most patients are attended by their own physicians while in hospice, if the so desire, there is

usually a hospice physician under contract to attend to special patient needs when their own physician is not available. While in hospice, only palliative care is given so physicians are not intended to order or perform curative therapy.

The Hospice Nurse

The first and foremost duty of hospice nursing is to provide pain and symptom control, give individualized care to each patient. They do all they can to promote comfort and quality of life to the patient and family. The main goal is to allow patient to die in comfortable surroundings and with dignity. In all cases, the family is included in the focus of patient care. Hospice nursing is more holistic and psychosocial focused than curative hospital care.

The Patient Care Coordinator

The role of patient care coordinator is to coordinate the team process and to act as a resource for pain and symptom control. He/she guides the hospice team to act within the hospice Medicare guidelines and the NHO standards to assure quality care delivery to hospice patients. The major goal is to promote quality of life for a very diverse terminally ill population and to promote excellence in hospice care delivery. It is the patient care coordinator's aim to provide holistic palliative care to the terminally ill patients. It is also the role of the patient care coordinator to provide hospice education to employees and the community. He/she is a liaison with hospitals, nursing homes and the community.

The Hospice Social Worker

The major role of the hospice social worker is to assure the patient's right to death with dignity and providing supportive counseling and assistance to the family. He/she is proficient in using community resources that will allow the patient and family maximum independence and life quality. As much as possible, the family is included in focus of patient care. The hospice social worker is usually specially trained in counseling to death and dying issues. He/she should be able to work well with the ill, disabled and emotionally disturbed people of all ages from all economic and cultural backgrounds in their home environment as well as in the hospice facility.

The Hospice Pastoral Counselor

Though patients and their families usually choose to have their own clergy visit and counsel them in hospice, most facilities have their own clergy available to counsel and aid their patients and the loved ones. The hospice chaplaincy philosophy requires that all faiths are to be respected and valued. Furthermore, religious activity and prayer is not forced on anyone not desiring such services. The chaplaincy affirms the right of every person to pursue their own spiritual path. The chaplaincy is available to accompany each person on his/her own spiritual journey and family is included if they so desire. Also bereavement work, either in anticipation or after the death, is an important component of the hospice chaplain's work. The hospice chaplain is often a liaison with local clergy.

They are available to aid the family in arranging funerals and memorial services and to council the bereaved. They often make home visits when requested.

The Hospice Bereavement Counselor

In addition to the hospice chaplaincy, there is often a bereavement coordinator or counselor to help support to the bereaved following their loss. The bereavement counselor can often best serve the bereaved by providing therapeutic listening, offering education and understanding related to the grief process and offer emotional support and encouragement for doing the difficult work of grief.

The Hospice Volunteer Coordinator

This may be one of the most important members of the hospice staff. Volunteers are among the most important staff of any hospice. Indeed many hospices could never function as efficiently as they do without their volunteer staff. It is the role of the volunteer coordinator to recruit, train, and support volunteers to provide their essential services. The volunteer coordinator must work well with a diverse population of volunteers. He/she must respect and understand each individual volunteer's motivations and needs to volunteering. The volunteer coordinator must train each volunteer to understand his/her need to be as involved in the dying process required by the individual patient. He/she must train volunteers to look at the patient's and his/her family's quality of life and comfort and their goal. Another important function of the volunteer coordinator is to give psychosocial support to volunteers so they are able to deal with dying patients and their loved ones.

The Hospice Volunteer Team

As mentioned above hospice volunteers are an essential part of the hospice staff. They are an amazing group of people making a very difficult job a labor of love. Hospice volunteers are often people who themselves have had loved ones pass through the hospice program and understand first hand the fear, anxiety, stress and grief that patients and the families go through. For this reason, they are often the most comforting members of the staff. Their main job is to give time and aid to the patients and their families and thus they may have the most interaction with the dying and their loved ones. They are the most remarkable of people.

Hospice Physical and Occupational Therapists

Many hospice facilities have staff physical and/or occupational therapists. It is their job to teach skills to the patient and their families to enhance their living, comfort, mobility and sense of independence and to promote quality of life remaining in the course of a terminal disease process. They help provide an environment that enhances patient safety and assist the patient in maintaining function and mobility. They help to promote the patient's self esteem and dignity.

They teach relaxation for pain and nausea control, help to decrease stress and increase the patient's energy. They implement training to caregivers for exercise, providing patient comfort, safety, body mechanics, conservation of energy, bed mobility and patient's night needs.

The Hospice Home Health Aide

Should home hospice care be selected, the hospice home health aide will provide care for patients under the direction and supervision of a registered nurse or physician. He/she will observe, record and report information about the patient's condition. The home health aide will help provide a clean, safe, and healthy environment. Other services which may be performed by the home health aide include providing respite care while primary caregiver is absent, assist the patient with bathing, toilet and personal hygiene, perform light housekeeping or meal preparation and if necessary run some errands.

These are the remarkable people who make up the very special staff of most hospices. Their jobs are often very difficult and in their brief interactions with the dying patients and their families they may develop special bonds which may lead to their own need for grief work. But it is because of their devotion to their difficult jobs that the patient's job of passing is made infinitely easier.

IX

Hospice Care for the Patient

It's all about the patient...

This and the next chapter are somewhat of reviews of the past chapters and are for the purpose of helping you decide between in hospice care and home hospice care. Don't be surprised by some redundancies. Remember, hospice care is all about the patient's needs, and though you should consider the limitations of family caregivers, the patient's needs and desires should be paramount in your decisions. As difficult a time this may be for family and loved ones, it is the patient's last days and the emphasis of decisions should on granting the patient's last wishes.

X

Hospice Care for the Family

Family, friends and loved ones will find support too...

When a family member or close friend is in hospice, it is usually a very stressful time for those keeping watch as the loved one lives out his/her final days. The hospice patient is more often than not resigned to the fact he/she is dying. In fact, the patient is in hospice by choice and as time passes, they begin to look forward to the transition from life to death. If the terminal illness has been very debilitating and painful, the patient will be anxious to have it over. Not so with family and friends.

Even when it is expected, when life passes it is a difficult time for the survivors. To lose a spouse, parent, sibling or a child can be devastating. For this reason, hospice programs are designed with the entire family and close friends as part of their treatment program. Virtually all the services available to the patient, baring medication, are available to family and close friends. The survivors are often in greater need of emotional support than the patient.

Social services, clergy, and volunteers will spend time with those in need, helping them better understand and prepare for the patient's passing. This can be especially helpful to prepare surviving children for the lose of parent, sibling, grandparent or other family or friend.

Furthermore, hospice care is available to the survivors after the passing to help with grief work and bereavement. Often hospices will offer support groups both during the patients stay as well as after to help the survivors. Some may offer widow and widower support groups as well as special support groups for children and teen survivors.

Often the hospice clergy is available to help plan memorial services and arrange funerals. Social workers will aid the family to straighten out financial problems caused by long illnesses and guide them through insurance mazes.

In both home and hospice facility care, one of the most important services to the family is respite care. The watching and waiting and care by the family and friends take their toll. Under the best of conditions and situations, caregiving family and friends have to get away from their vigil for at least brief periods. Whether for just a brief walk, necessary shopping, to spend some time with the kids, just to get out for a few minutes or hours, you've just got to get out and away to revitalize and put aside your vigil. But to do this without increasing concern and worry, you have to have confidence that the patient is safe and in good hands. Hospice offers home aides and trained volunteers to provide this care in your absence either at home or in the hospice facility.

Hospice has a great deal to offer families and friends of the patient and they willingly will give you any help you may need. Take advantage of their expertise.

XI

Hospice Care for Children

Care and support for the child patient or the child survivor of a dying parent or loved one...

Too often hospice care for children is an unfulfilled need. Probably because young children are not supposed to get terminally ill or to die, however they do. Sadly, each year well over 50,000 children die in the United States. Worldwide, it is estimated over seven million children and their families could benefit from children's hospice palliative care. Yet less than one percent of children who could benefit from hospice care in the United States receive it.

Thanks to Children's Hospice International, an organization dedicated raising awareness for the need of children's hospices, the number of children receiving hospice and palliative care is on the raise. It is sad but true that children of all ages are not immune to terminal illness and lingering death. Children's hospice care eases the child's fears and discomfort and supports parents, siblings, relatives and close friends in their emotional strain and grief.

It is not surprising that most children's hospice in carried out in home care. A family faced with a child's terminal illness is kept together whenever possible and in most cases it is best to keep children in their own familiar, loving home environment. Each family's social, emotional, spiritual as well as financial and other needs should be evaluated and professional support should be supplied to meet these needs.

A survey in 1999 disclosed 379 known hospice programs worldwide that accepted children. Many existing hospice programs are willing to consider accepting children into their programs if the pediatric expertise needed were available. Children's hospice care makes every effort to prepare parents to assume the role of primary caregivers. The comprehensive hospice care for children provides coordinated home care, and inpatient care through the same interdisciplinary team used in adult care, but which is coordinated by a qualified pediatric physician and registered nurse. Along with trained volunteers, the team provides medical, psychological, social, and spiritual care to patient and family. Hospice care for children strives to be attentive to family needs related to loss and grieving both prior to as well as following a death.

The hospice clergy can be of great help in preparing siblings to understand what is happening in the family. As painful as it is for parents to see their children seriously ill, it is even harder for children if they do not have the illness or death of a loved one explained to them. It is better for a child to mourn included in the company of family than to mourn alone, wondering and afraid to ask questions. As a parent, you should take the lead by explaining and request the help of hospice staff to answer the child's questions as best you can. Encourage the children to ask questions, and be prepared to give honest and simple answers. Encourage them to ask questions as they arise, and to express their feelings and thoughts. Reassure other children in the family that you love them even though you will be giving more attention to the child with the illness.

XII

Being a Caregiver

One of the hardest jobs you'll ever have...

Being an effective caregiver is not just taking care of
the physical needs of a terminal patient. You will not
only find yourself doing what seems like unending
physical chores, but the emotional demands on you will
be daunting. It is stressful to the extreme caring for a
loved one, spouse, sibling, child or close friend who is
dying. It will indeed probably be one of the most
difficult tasks you will ever have to face in your life
time. Caregiving is a tremendously challenging job and
you should depend on the help offered by hospice to
the fullest.

You and your patient must not only deal with the
physical effects of his/her disease and the medications
prescribed for relief of pain and symptoms, but also
the psychological challenges of knowing that this
illness is imminently terminal. You must do your best
to support the patient's efforts to deal with the reality
of his/her prognosis. At the same time, you will have

to come to terms with your own feelings, fears and emotions toward your impending loss of a loved one. Hard as it may be, you should support the patient's efforts to live as normal a remaining life as is possible

Terminal patients often want to talk about things never before or rarely previously expressed. Let your patient talk about whatever he/she wants and encourage them to get whatever it may be with whomever he/she wants. Likewise be willing to express your innermost feelings as long as they are not meant to hurt. People who have never talked much about their feelings at these times find it necessary and comforting to express themselves fully. Listening patiently and carefully and letting your patient know that you understand what he/she is trying to express is important.

People with terminal illness will naturally become anxious over their symptoms, their death or even your future. Encourage them to express their feelings, fears and worries so you can help them cope and reassure them. Feel free to seek advice from your hospice staff on how to help the patient cope with his/her depressed thoughts, feelings and worries. Do your best to avoid conflicts. Disagreements are bound to occur, but consider what is really important. Avoid the minor conflicts and fully discuss issues that really count.

Encourage the patient to express his/her needs, desires and wishes. Let the patient participate in decisions and make as many decisions as possible. Taking away your patient's ability to make decisions can undermine his/her feelings of worth. It is important that you don't increase the patient's feelings of helplessness. Let them know and feel that they still have control of themselves and their future.

Don't be surprised if your patient becomes deeply concerned over spiritual matters. Even people who have shown little interest in such matters in the past may raise fundamental questions about life, why are we here and wondering if they've led a good life. They may wonder for the first time about what happens after death. Encourage the patient's discussion of these matters and if helpful, don't hesitate to invite the hospice clergy or your own spiritual leader into these discussions.

When the end of life nears, patients commonly to want to take actions or have certain experiences before they die; to do or see something important or pleasant once more. Often it is simply to say things to someone that has been left unsaid in the past or to resolve old misunderstandings. Make what reasonable attempts you can to arrange for satisfaction of these desires. Weigh their importance to the patient against the cost and possibility of satisfying their wishes; if arrangements can't be made, explain the situation with the patient fully.

Don't try to do everything yourself; ask for help. At times like this friends want to help, so let them. Depend on your hospice staff. Let your needs be known to other family members, your friends, clergy and acquaintances. Utilize the hospice staff to help train other caregivers willing to help you. All the people willing to help you have to be told how to do what is needed. You need to make clear to these people about what you would like them to do and how to carry out their duties.

Above all, you have to be at your best if you are to provide the good care to your patient. You must pay attention to your own needs. Set limits on what you can expect yourself to do. Take time off to care for yourself. Utilize hospice staff and friends to give yourself respite time. Make sure you get adequate sleep, eat well and exercise. Go for frequent walks. If you are used to going to the gym, make sure you arrange time to keep up with that routine. It will keep you well and help from letting you fall into a deep depressions. You can't properly care for your loved one if you don't properly care for yourself.

As caregiver, you may be called upon to make serious decisions. Don't make them when you are overwhelmed or upset. If you have doubts about your decisions, ask for help and advice. You have the hospice staff to help you and they probably have vast experience among them to advise you. Discuss problems with friends you respect or seek professional help.

While your loved one is in hospice, it is natural for you to run the gamut of human emotions, anger, fear, sadness, guilt, joy at pleasant memories, bitterness at the situation; a rollercoaster of feelings. Again, rely on your hospice staff to discuss your own feelings, or seek out friends, relatives or clergy you respect and trust to listen to your feelings and help you cope. Discuss your feelings of loss with others who have had similar experiences. Especially people who have been caregivers will understand how you feel. Many hospices provide support groups for caregivers where you can express your feelings and vent your own pent up emotions.

Being caregiver to a terminal patient is perhaps the greatest sign of love you can express to someone. Take what comfort you can from that thought. Don't try or expect to be perfect, just sincere. Do the best you can and ask for help when needed.

XIII

After It's Over

No matter how prepared you are, you're never ready...

No matter how long your vigil has been, when the end finally comes it will probably be a shock. My wife was in hospice for 12 weeks slowly slipping away. The last weeks she hardly ate anything and only took sips of water given her by syringe. No one could understand how she held on for so long. We were all prepared to see her pass on weeks before. However when the end came it was still a shock. It had been hard to believe she could have held on so long, it was even harder to believe she was gone when she finally did pass on.

That shock and disbelief is likely to stay with you for days. You may be in your living room and find yourself expecting your departed loved one to be in the kitchen or out shopping or find yourself waiting for him/her to come home from work. If it's your spouse that died you'll likely feel your only half of yourself. If you've been married for a long time you'll come to realize that you've seen yourself not as an individual but half of the whole that made up you as a couple. You can expect to face the deepest loneliness you've ever experienced. Spend as much time as you can with family, friends and acquaintances as you can.

That first week after your loved ones passing will seem surreal. There will be lots of things you will have to take care of during the days after that first week such as financial matters, social security, insurance, legal matters … and as difficult as that may be, it will help take your mind off of your loss to some degree. But the evenings and nights will be the most difficult. Expect it. But also keep in mind that life will go on and it will get better. This is all part of normal bereavement. Consider getting into a support group. Others who have been through what you will be suffering can be a great help in coping with your own situation and grief. Grief work is tough, but it is essential and normal. Let your hospice help you through this difficult time.

The next chapter will help you to better understand bereavement and grief and their importance to recapturing a new productive and happy life.

XIV

Bereavement

Grief is a difficult job, but you mustn't avoid it... and don't forget the kids...

Grief is a necessary and normal response of sorrow, emotion, and confusion, despair, helplessness, denial and anger that comes from losing someone dear to you. It is a natural part healing and life. Grief is a typical and universal reaction to death. Following a death, a person will most likely feel empty and numb and in shock. There are frequent physical changes with trembling, nausea, trouble breathing such as shortness of breath or hyperventilation, muscle weakness, lightheadedness, dry mouth, or trouble sleeping and eating. You may become overwhelmed with anger - at the situation, at a particular person, at God, or even at the person who has died for leaving you, or just angry in general. Expect to experiences guilt; guilt expressed at what you could have done, should have done, wish you would have done differently. Even if you know you couldn't have done more, you will still question emotionally if you did all you could have.

While grieving you may have nightmares, find you're absent-minded, withdraw socially, and lack the desire to return to work or do much of anything. These feelings and accompanying behaviors are normal and almost universal during grief. Take heart, they will pass. Grief can pass in a few weeks or last for years; lasting as long as it takes you to accept your loss emotionally and resign yourself to live with it.

Every person who experiences a death must eventually accept the loss, work through the physical and emotional pain of their grief; adjust themselves to living in a world without the person they've lost; and finally move on with life.

Normal grief usually involves at least two or more of Elisabeth Kubler-Ross' 5 grief stages: in usual sequential order, are denial, anger, bargaining, depression, and acceptance.

Childhood bereavement differs from that of adults. The loss of a parent, grandparent or sibling may be extremely troubling to a child. Furthermore, within childhood, there are age differences in relation to the response to loss. Childhood loss can predispose a child to physical illness as well as to severe emotional problems and an increased risk for suicide, especially in the adolescent years. It is essential that you pay close attention to a child's response to grief and seek professional intervention if grief brings about major changes in the child's behavior.

When a child dies, parents almost always find the grief unbearably devastating. The death of a child is perhaps one of the most intense forms of grief.

Intervention and comforting support can make all the difference to the survival of a parent in this type of grief but it still may cause family breakup or suicide. Even in the event of a miscarriage, it is important for friends and family members to acknowledge the loss of the pregnancy, and not to attempt to minimize the significance of the loss.

Even when the death of a spouse is expected after a long illness or as we age, it is a particularly powerful loss of a loved-one. A spouse frequently becomes a significant part of the partner in a special and unique way. Often widows and widowers describe the death of a spouse as losing a half of themselves. After a long marriage, the elderly may find it a very difficult to begin a new life alone. Social isolation may also take place as the survivor may find it difficult to function comfortably in groups composed mainly of couples. When queried about what in life is most tragic most rate the experience of the death of a spouse the worst.

XV

Facing Life

After the grief has been worked through engage in the renewed life your loved one would want you to live....

This chapter is taken from "When Your Spouse Dies ... a widow's and widower's handbook" by Othniel Seiden, MD and Jane Bilett, PhD, A Boomer Book Series book. www.boomerbookseries.com ISBN: 0-9801941-6-4

DON'T FORGET YOUR SOCIAL NEEDS

We humans are social animals. Don't repress your own social needs. You must interact with people of your own age and interests. You can't spend your life with only your family. Break out of the stereotype of an odd number at the table.

After a reasonable time, you have every right to a social life of your own. What that reasonable time limit is - is strictly up to you. You'll know when you're ready. To some it may be a few weeks to others perhaps a year more or less. You are a living human being and as such are a social animal. Social animal does not only mean you have a right to a social life of your own, it means you need a social life of your own. You must get out and do the things you are interested in. You must have social interaction with other humans outside of your immediate family circle. Yes, you may have added responsibilities to your children if they are still in the home but this does not mean you should repress your own social needs. Quite the contrary!

You must interact with people of your own age and interests for those who depend on you as well as for yourself. You can't spend your life with only your family. This can only breed resentment, anger, hostile feelings, depression and unhappiness for everyone. Make time for yourself to get out daily to do things you want to do and do them with others as often as possible.

Do not let yourself become stereotyped as the odd number at the table as so many widows and widowers do. Let people know that your are interested in being matched up with other single persons at dinner parties, card games, concerts and other cultural and social events. Remember, one of the best ways to get invitations is to invite. What better way to let people know you are ready to socialize than to extend an invitation to a dinner party or social event of your own. If you don't feel able to throw a party yourself, arrange an evening out with a few friends to a restaurant, show or concert or wherever else you'd like to go with acquaintances. For you to host a party is no way disrespect to your departed spouse.

Not only do you need to renew old acquaintances, you should make new friend, people of similar interests, both men and women. For some, meeting new people is a difficult task. You have to work at it. To do this you must get out where those people are. Let's list a few places to consider:

The work place

The work place may or may not be a good place for you to make new social contacts. Certainly most jobs expose you to many new people and often people of similar interests. But there may also be problems caused by socializing with customers, clients, superiors and sometimes co-workers. Determine what the policies of your firm are. Be especially cautious if you work for a physician, law firm, accounting firm and plan to become socially involved with patients or clients. Also keep in mind that if you get socially involved with a superior and the relationship goes sour, you may also find yourself out of a job. The safest way to use the work place as a source for new social contacts is to take up with co-workers or use them as a source of introductions to outsiders.

Health clubs

In recent years, health clubs have become an excellent place to meet new friends. At the same time you may get yourself back into shape. A health club is probably a safer and more reliable place to meet people than the singles bar scene. Shop around and you should be able to find a club that fits your budget. If you figure up what you'd spend at singles bars, you'll probably consider the health club a bargain and far better for you physically. The people you meet there are more likely to be healthier than those you meet elsewhere, certainly a positive characteristic.

Organizations

There are an unlimited number organizations for people of all interests. Get involved in one or several that offer you opportunities to do volunteer work, pursue hobby interests, further your profession or whatever. You should meet others who share similar values and interests with you. That's the stuff friendships are made of. "I've always been interested in politics," a young widow told me. "When a neighbor asked me if I'd be interested in joining her at a neighborhood caucus meeting I said, 'yes.' Not only was it interesting for me, but I met several people who I really enjoyed. At that same meeting, they asked for volunteer campaign workers. My hand went up before I even thought about it. That led me to meet numerous other people. Over the next few months, I found a whole new group of acquaintances and at least three close friends. My life has started in a whole new direction. I love it...."

Church

If you have a religious affiliation or leanings, look to church, mosque or synagogue for a source of new friends and acquaintances. Get involved in the activities of your institution. They probably need all the help they can get and in return you should be rewarded by many new and stimulating relationships.

Classes and Adult Continuing Education

What can be better than to develop your mind, expanding your horizons at the same time that you meet new and interesting people? Most colleges, public schools and private corporations established for the purpose now offer courses, seminars and workshops for adults who want to broaden their knowledge. You may want to work toward a degree or just pursue latent interests. In either case, consider your classes as ideal places to meet new friends.

By the way, if you haven't noticed over the past few years, the demographics of the average college have changed dramatically. Over 50% of college students today are women. A large percentage of students are married, widowed or divorced. Many colleges state that the average ages of their students are between 25 and 50 years of age. There are almost as many students with graying hair in our colleges as there are youngsters. The point is that you won't be out of place in any classes you take, regardless of your age or circumstances.

Friends and Family

Let your acquaintances know you want to meet new people. Encourage them to include you in gatherings where you don't necessarily know everyone. Chances are a potential best friend for you is someone who is already a casual acquaintance of someone you already know.

Advertise

Don't gasp at the suggestion and don't laugh!

This is getting to be one of the more common ways to meet new and interesting friends. Look through the personal ads in some of the most prestigious publications. Those people are not joking. You can either advertise for someone of specific qualities and interests or you can answer an ad that sounds like you. If you advertise, do not publish your phone number, address or name. If the publication does not offer a reply service by code number, do not place your ad. Taking proper precautions to keep your identity confidential can produce numerous legitimate introductions for you to very nice people who are looking for the same thing you are, new friendships with people of similar likes and needs.

One widower in a support group stated to everyone's surprise, "I have answered several ads in the personal column of our newspaper. At first, I was just curious and dropped a note to a woman who described her interests as similar to mine. I sent it to a box number at the paper. It included a brief description of me and a number where she could reach me if she was interested. To be frank with you, I was surprised when I got her call five days later. I was also surprised at how nice she sounded on the phone. She invited me to meet her on the next Saturday afternoon at the coffee shop at the Museum Of Natural History. It was a safe place for her and I guess for me too. The whole thing turned into a delightful afternoon. We've since taken in several concerts and a show or two. We've both found a friend in each other. I've answered two other ads like that. Nothing came of either of them, but one out of three isn't at all bad."

The Internet

Yes, the computer age is here and with it there are numerous computer dating services. Actually the computer is an ideal matchmaker. How do they work? Computers can store and sort enormous quantities of information. You will be given a questionnaire to fill out which should go into great detail as to your likes, dislikes, interests, needs, quirks, pet peeves, long and short term social goals, etc. This information will go into a computer where it should be kept very confidential. However, it will be able to match you up with individuals who have similar purposes without revealing your more intimate details. When the computer makes a match you will be given just enough information to let you decide if you want to be introduced. If both parties agree, an introduction will be made in as un-stressful and safe a situation as possible. Computer dating is as safe and good as the organization offering the service. Take the time to investigate and shop around to determine which service is best for you.

Othniel and Jane met on an internet dating program about a year and a half after I became a widower. She was the ninth date I met through the service, about two months after I started with the program. Shop around for the best cost and contract. If the service is on the up-and-up and within your budget, go for it!

We highly recommend it!

Tours

If you like to travel and can afford one of the many tours available through travel agencies, churches, schools and organizations, this is a delightful way to meet and make new friends. If you shop around, you can find tours that are designed for very specific groups such as singles tours, over fifties tours, cultural interest tours, educational tours or just general tours for anyone interested in seeing specific places.

Check around with the travel agents in your area. Remember, travel agents make their money from the airlines, hotels and tour companies so you shouldn't have to pay them for their services. A good travel agent can save you lots of troubles and find you the perfect vacation for your needs.

Singles bars

You are probably not the singles bars type. Singles bars cater more to the never married, the divorced or married people on the prowl. If, on the other hand, you felt at home in the bar scene before your spouse died then the singles bar might be where you can most comfortably meet new people. We are here neither to judge you nor refer you to the singles bars. Just be careful!

The above is far from a complete list of where you can make new friends and acquaintances to expand your social network. It should, however, prove to you that there are many ways for you to expand your relationships - as many ways as a little creativity and ingenuity can dream up. If you feel you can't meet new people, I suggest you take a hard look at your own motivation. Where the real will to meet people exists, there are numerous, very appropriate ways to get the job done.

ABOUT THE AUTHOR(S)
OTHNIEL J. SEIDEN, M.D.
JANE L. BILETT, PH.D.

Dealing with death is all too often required of physicians and clinical psychologists, but when Othniel J. Seiden, MD himself had to face a hospice experience with his first wife, he realized first hand the problems soon-to-be widows and widowers have to face and cope with.

With the help and collaboration of his new wife, clinical psychologist Jane L. Bilett, Ph.D., he was able to successfully re-travel this difficult road to share his insights both as a physician and a husband.

It is with the experiences that Drs. Bilett and Seiden plus both of their professional and clinical experiences that made them an ideal couple team to write this handbook for anyone who has to face hospice for themselves or a loved one..

This book not only forewarns its readers of the obstacles in the rough road ahead through the hospice experience, but helps to smooth those ruts in the path through the authors' own trial and error experiences.

OTHER BOOKS BY SEIDEN & BILETT

OTHNIEL SEIDEN, MD & JANE BILETT, PhD

HEAVY & HEALTHY - THORNTON PUBLISHING 2007 -- BOOMER BOOK SERIES **ISBN: 0-9779960-5-0**

SEX IN THE GOLDEN YYEARS - THORNTON PUBLISHING 2007 - BOOMER BOOK SERIES **ISBN: 0-9801941-0-5**

THE SECOND HALF BEGINS AT 50 - THORNTON PUBLISHING 2007 - BOOMER BOOK SERIES **ISBN: 0-9801941-1-3**

QUIT SMOKING NOW! THORNTON PUBLISHING SPONSORED BY DOCTORS TO THE WORLD

WHEN YOUR SPOUSE DIES - THORNTON PUBLISHING - 2008 - BOOMER BOOK SERIES **ISBN: 0-9801941-6-4**

THE HOSPICE EXPERIENCE - THORNTON PUBLISHING - 2008 - BOOMER BOOK SERIES **ISBN: 0-9801941-5-6**

SHARPENING THE AGING MIND - THORNTON PUBLISHING - 2008 - BOOMER BOOK SERIES **ISBN: 0-9801941-7-2**

THE JOY OF VOLUNTEERING - THORNTON PUBLISHING - 2008 - BOOMER BOOK SERIES **COMING IN 2008**

HISTORICAL NOVELS BY OTHNIEL SEIDEN

THE CARTOGRAPHER..1492 - THORNTON PUBLISHING 2007 BOOMER BOOK SERIES **ISBN: 0-9801941-2-1**

THE REMNANT - THORNTON PUBLISHING - 2008 BOOMER BOOK SERIES **ISBN: 0-9801941-4-8**

THE SURVIVOR OF BABI YAR -- STONEHENGE 1981

THE CAPUCHIN -- GREGORY HILL PUBLICATIONS 1982

SEED OF ABRAHAM - THORNTON PUBLISHING - 2008 BOOMER BOOK SERIES **COMING IN 2008**

NON-FICTION BY OTHNIEL J. SEIDEN

SO YOU WANT TO WRITE A BOOK - THORNTON PUBLISHING - 2008 ISBN: 0-9801941-3-X

DENVER'S RICHTHOFEN CASTLE -- STONEHENGE 1980
BUFFALO BILL: HIS LIFE AND LEGEND -- STONEHENGE 1981
YOUR AIR FORCE ACADEMY -- R.M.W.G. PUBLICATIONS 1982
COPING WITH MISCARRIAGE -- TAB BOOKS 1984
COPING WITH YOUR BAD BACK -- TAB BOOKS 1984
COPING WITH DIABETES -- TAB BOOKS 1984
WALK - GET INTO SHAPE THE EASY WAY -- TAB BOOKS 1984
LET'S LEARN YIDDISH -- DTTW PRODUCTIONS 1987 -- LANGUAGE COURSE.
HEALTHWALK -- FULCRUM 1988
FIFTY PLUS-- HEALTH - TAYLOR PUBLISHING 1997
PROPECIA-THE HAIR REPLACEMENT BREAKTHROUGH (2 LANGUAGES)-PRIMA PUBLISHING -1998
VIAGRA - THE VIRILITY BREAKTHROUGH (4 LANGUAGES)- PRIMA PUBLISHING -- 1998
5-HTP...THE SEROTONIN CONNECTION - PRIMA PUBLISHING -- 1998
MERIDIA...THE WEIGHT-LOSS BREAKTHROUGH (2 LANGUAGES) - PRIMA PUBLISHING - 1998

ALL BOOKS STILL IN PRINT
AVAILABLE ON
BOOMERBOOKSERIES.COM

OR

AMAZON.COM

RECOMMENDED READING

On Death and Dying by Elisabeth Kubler-Ross

Final Gifts: Understanding the Special Awareness, Needs and Communications of the Dying by Maggie Callanan and Patricia Kelley

Ethnic Variations in Dying, Death and Grief by Donald P. Irish and Kathleen F. Lundquist

Questions and Answers on Death and Dying by Elisabeth Kubler-Ross

Understanding Dying, Death and Bereavement by Michael R. Leming and George E. Dickenson

The Sacred Art of Dying: How the World Religions Understand Death by Kenneth Kramer

I'm Grieving as Fast as I Can: How Young Widows and Widowers Can Cope and Heal by Linda Feinberg

The Widow's Financial Survival Guide by Nancy Dunnan

Starting Over: Help for Young Widows and Widowers by Adele Rice Nudel

Single wisdom: Empowering Singles, Divorcees, Widows and Widowers for Living a Purposeful Life.... by Paris M. Finner-Williams

Finding Your Way After Your Souse Dies by Marta Felber

The After Journey: Getting Through the First Year by Laury-Ann Weis

Comfort and Hope for Widows and Widowers by Donnette R. Alfelt

A Guidebook for Widows and Widowers: All the wise and Wherefores by Jessyca Russel Gaver

Marital Secrets: Dating, Lies, Communication and Sex by Paris Finner-Williams

Angel On Board by EJ Thornton ISBN: 1-932344-76-4

ORDER FORM
The Hospice Experience

$14.95 + 2.50 (S&H)

online at:
http://www..BoomerBookSeries.com

by phone:
have your credit card handy and call:
(303) 794-8888

by fax:
(720) 863-2013

by mail:
send check payable to:
Thornton Publishing, Inc.
17011 Lincoln Ave. #408
Parker, Colorado 80134

If it is temporarily sold out at your favorite bookstore,
have them order more of ISBN: 0-9801941-5-6

Name: _____

Address: _____

_____

Phone: _____

E-mail: _____

Credit Card #: _____

Card Type: _____ Expiration Date: ____/ ____

Security Code: _____

Printed in Great Britain
by Amazon.co.uk, Ltd.,
Marston Gate.